JUAN QUEZADA

As Told to Shelley Dale By Juan Quezada

Illustrated by Shelley Dale

"Así es como sucedió"

"This is how it happened"

Juan Quezada

NORMAN BOOKS

Santa Monica, CA

This is a true story. It is the story of how one curious and determined boy changed the future of his poor, nearly abandoned village in Northern Chihuahua, Mexico. Today the boy, Juan Quezada Celado, is a famous artist. His village of Mata Ortiz, a village of potters, is known all over the world. In 1999, the President of Mexico awarded Juan "el Premio Nacional de Ciencias y Artes (The National Award in Science and Arts)," for his revival of the ancient ceramic art of the Casas Grandes culture. This is the highest honor an artist in Mexico can receive.

"Tell the story about the special day, *Abuelito!*" begged Chato.

"Again?" asked Chato's grandfather Juan. "I told it to you last week."

"*Abuelita,* make him tell it!"

Grandmother *Guille* was burnishing one of her husband's painted clay pots with a *chilicote* bean. She gestured with her head toward two piles of smoldering ashes. Under one pile, covered by a clay *quemador,* was *Abuelito*'s hot, fired *olla grande.* Under the other, the first *ollita* Chato had made all by himself.

"Juan, you have time to tell the story while your *ollas* are cooling," said *Abuelita.* "You know Chato will keep asking until you do."

"I can begin," offered Chato. "One day..."

Abuelito laughed. He lifted his *sombrero* and smoothed his hair. He put on his *sombrero*, and pulled it down snugly.

"This is how it happened," he began. "When I was about thirteen years old, I collected firewood with my *burro*, Minuto. I'd bring home *piñones,* honey, anything to help feed our family of twelve."

"We'd see *ruinas* from the ancient peoples. There were large cooking pits where they boiled the *agave* plant into syrup. I'd find shards, broken pieces of hard, baked clay. Some were blackened from cooking fires, but others had beautiful colors. I wanted to know how the ancients had made this colored *barro*.

"I already knew how to make shapes from the sticky dirt near *el rio*," continued *Abuelito*. "When I put my dried shapes into *el fuego*, they would harden, like the shards, but they blew apart. Why? It was a mystery. Even the old people in our *pueblo* didn't remember how to make painted clay *ollas*."

"You became an *investigador*, didn't you?" asked Chato.

"*Si.*" *Abuelito* nodded. "I love to experiment. I began to throw everything I found into *el fuego: barro rojo*, colored rocks, white bones. I was searching for the secret of the colored *barro*."

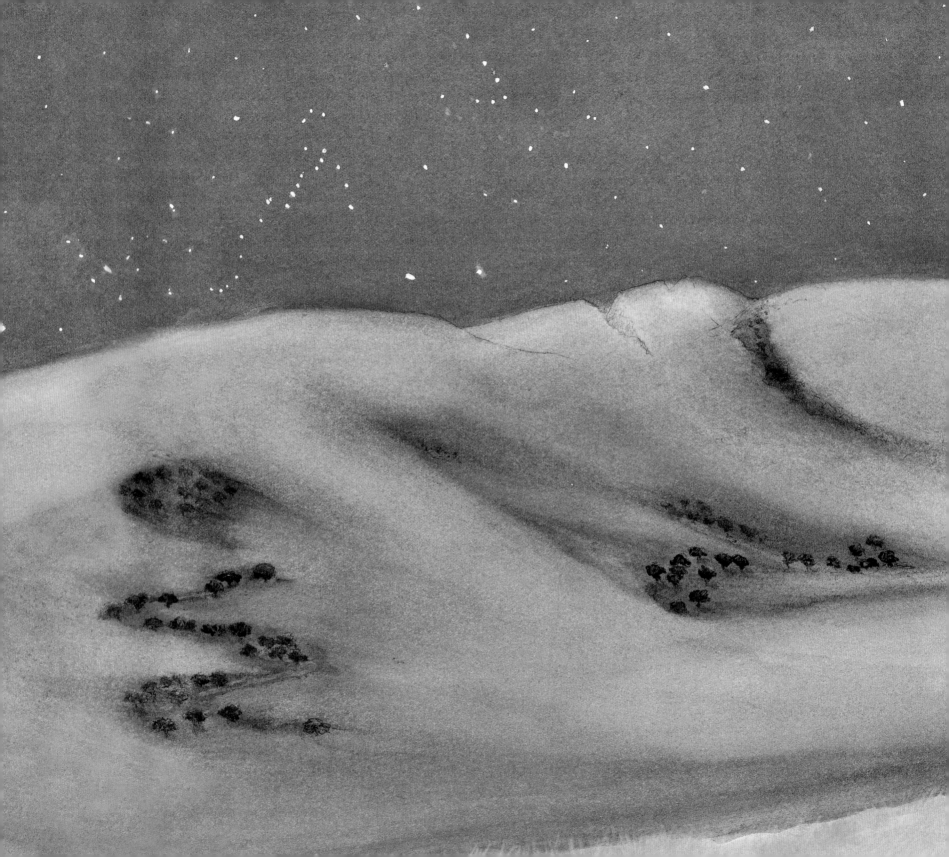

Abuelito paused, remembering many
nights in his beloved mountains.

"Then one day," prodded Chato.

"I forget," teased *Abuelito.*

"While Minuto was eating..." said Chato.

"I went exploring," said Abuelito.

"Hidden in a wall of rocks, I saw...."

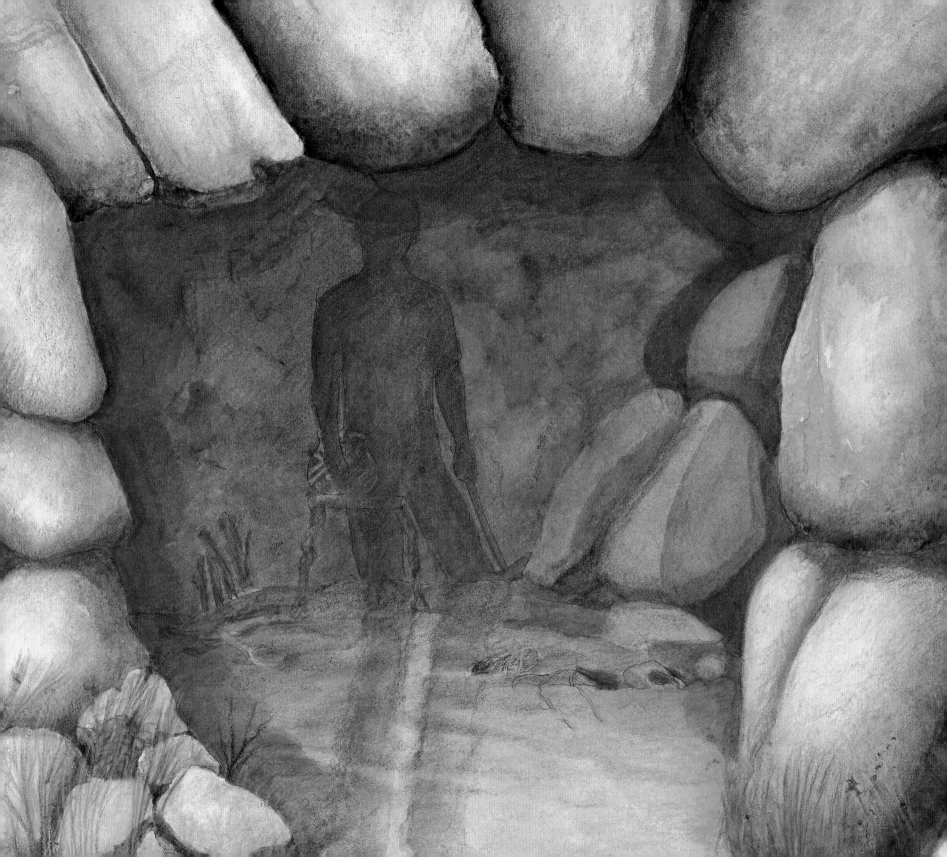

"A *cueva!*" whispered Chato.

"Who could resist a *cueva?*" asked *Abuelito.*

"Not my *Abuelito!*" said Chato.

"Inside the *cueva* I found a three-legged stool, a *calabaza* cup, pieces of woven *yucca zapatos* and..." *Abuelito* took a deep breath.

"An *olla!*" shouted Chato.

"*Sí.* And, it wasn't broken!" said *Abuelito.* "White spots marched around the *olla.* It was painted with the same colors and *diseños* as the shards I'd found in the *ruinas.* The *olla* must have been sitting on that stool for at least five hundred years. I put my hand inside the *olla.* I placed my fingertips in the marks left by the ancient *alfarero.* At that moment, I knew I had to find the secret of making an *olla* like this *pinta,* even if it took all of my life.

"I tried many ways to make an *olla.* Eventually, I used my mother's bowl to keep the bottom of my *ollita* from collapsing. I put a *tortilla* of *barro* inside her bowl. Then, I could add a fat *chorizo* of *barro* to the top edge of the *tortilla,* and pinch it taller."

Abuelito sighed. "Still, everything I made blew apart in *el fuego*."

"Why didn't you give up?" asked Chato.

"I listened to the stone chips and shards crunching under my feet," answered *Abuelito*. "They told me other boys had lived here long ago, making arrowheads and *ollas*. If they had figured it out, so could I."

"You needed a clue," suggested Chato.

"And I found it," replied *Abuelito*. "The shards I'd found near *el rio* were stronger than the others. I looked at them again. Something gritty was in them. What could it be?"

"Sand!" yelled Chato.

"*Si!*" said *Abuelito.* "When I added sand from the river, my *ollas* stopped cracking. Later, I found other *barro rojo* on the ranch of Manuel Lopez, and mixed it with sand. That was the first *olla* I liked. By that time, I was already eighteen. But it took many more years of searching and experimenting to find the *barros* and *pinturas* we use today."

Chato giggled. "You made a paintbrush with fur from a squirrel's tail!"

"Why not? I wanted to paint my own *diseños.* I tried bird feathers, cactus spines, and dog's fur, too," said *Abuelito.*

"And don't forget my plants," added *Abuelita.*

"*Sí,*" admitted *Abuelito.* "Then, when I used several strands of a young girl's hair, my painting flowed like breathing."

"*Abuelito,*" said Chato, "We forgot! Spencer comes before the paintbrush."

Guille poked her husband lightly. "Juan," she teased, "maybe we should let our *nieto* Chato tell the story next time."

"I know what's next," said Chato. He knocked on the tree three times with his fist. "*Uno, dos, tres,*" he counted.

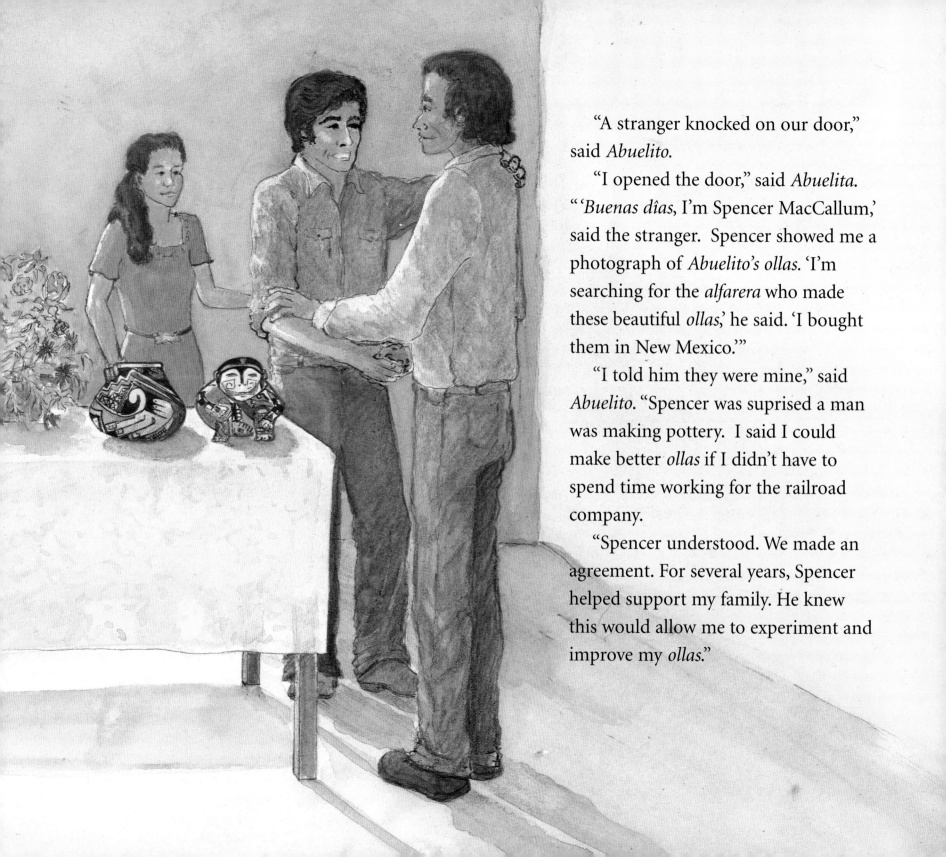

"A stranger knocked on our door," said *Abuelito*.

"I opened the door," said *Abuelita*. "'*Buenas dîas*, I'm Spencer MacCallum,' said the stranger. Spencer showed me a photograph of *Abuelito's ollas*. 'I'm searching for the *alfarera* who made these beautiful *ollas*,' he said. 'I bought them in New Mexico.'"

"I told him they were mine," said *Abuelito*. "Spencer was suprised a man was making pottery. I said I could make better *ollas* if I didn't have to spend time working for the railroad company.

"Spencer understood. We made an agreement. For several years, Spencer helped support my family. He knew this would allow me to experiment and improve my *ollas*."

"Spencer took *Abuelito's* pots to museums," said *Abuelita*. "When people saw his beautiful work, they held exhibits. Schools invited *Abuelito* to teach."

"I taught my brother Nicolás to make *ollas*," said *Abuelito*. "And my sisters, Consolacíon and Reynalda. We taught anyone who wanted to learn. When we earned money making *ollas*, families who'd left our *pueblo* to find work came home to learn pottery."

"I'm learning too, aren't I, *Abuelito*?" asked Chato.

"*Sí*, you will be a fine *alfarero*," said *Abuelito*. "Come, it's time to look at our *ollas*."

Abuelito lifted the *grande quemador* that was covering his pot. Chato lifted his *quemador*.

"*Mira, Abuelita*," said Chato.

"That's a beautiful *ollita*," said *Abuelita*.

"It certainly is, Chato," said *Abuelito*. "Let's have a closer look at our work."

Abuelito Juan picked up his *olla grande* and held it high.

Chato picked up his *ollita* and held it high.

"The day I found the *olla pinta* in the *cueva* was special, Chato," said *Abuelito*. "It changed the lives of everyone in our *pueblo*. But making *ollas* with my *nieto*, this is truly a special day."

GLOSSARY

(Phonetic prounciation. Stress mark is at the beginning of the stressed syllable)

Abuelita	*a bway 'lee tah*	Grandmother
Abuelito	*a bway 'lee toe*	Grandfather
agave	*a 'gah veh*	a plant [cooked into sweet paste in ancient times]
alfarera	*ahl fa 'ray rah*	a female potter
alfarero	*ahl fa 'ray row*	a male potter
barro	*'bah rroh*	clay
bueno	*'bway no*	good, ok!
buenas días	*'bway nos 'dee has*	hello! Good morning!
Chato	*'Chat oh*	Family nickname for Orlando Quinta Quezada
chilicote	*chee lee 'coh tay*	a smooth bean [used to polish Juan's pottery]
chorizo	*kor 'ree so*	sausage: a thick coil of clay
cueva	*'kway vah*	a cave
diseño	*dee 'sayn yo*	a design
dos	*dohs*	two
el	*"L"*	the
fuego	*fway go*	fire
grande	*'grahn day*	big
Guille	*'Gee yay*	(G as in good) nickname for Guillermina, Juan's wife

investigador	*een ves tee gah 'door*	investigator
mano	*'mah no*	grinding stone held in hand
metate	*meh 'tah tay*	grinding dish made of stone
molde	*'mohl day*	a mold or dish, [to support the bottom of a clay pot]
mira	*'meer ah*	look!
nieta (f)	*nee 'eh tah*	grandaughter
nieto (m)	*nee 'eh tow*	grandson
olla	*'oy yah*	a clay pot
ollita	*oy 'yee tah*	small pot
piñones	*peen 'yoh nays*	edible pine nuts
pinta	*'peen tah*	ancient spotted pots, Casas Grandes style
pinturas	*peen 'toor ahs*	mineral paints; [colors]
pueblo	*'pweh blo*	village
quemador	*kay mah 'door*	bucket used to cover pots while firing
rojo	*'roh ho*	red
ruinas	*'roo ee nahs*	pre-Columbian ruin
si	*see*	yes
tortilla	*tor 'tee yah*	flat corn pancake
tres	*trace*	three
una (f) uno (m)	*'oo nah*	a, an, one

HISTORY

Mesoamerica and the Gran Chichimeca

The central part of Mexico is referred to as "Mesoamerica." It extends from the Gulf of Mexico to the Pacific Coast and from the tropical jungles in the south to the Tropic of Cancer on the edge of Mexico's northern deserts. Since pre-historic times this area has been the heartland of the sophisticated Mexican cultures, an area where art and commerce flourished. North of the Tropic of Cancer lived the Chichimec people, which means the "sons of dogs." They roamed the wild deserts hunting animals and gathering seeds and plants to eat. The vast, rugged territory of the Chichimec people became known as the "Gran Chichimeca." It extended north

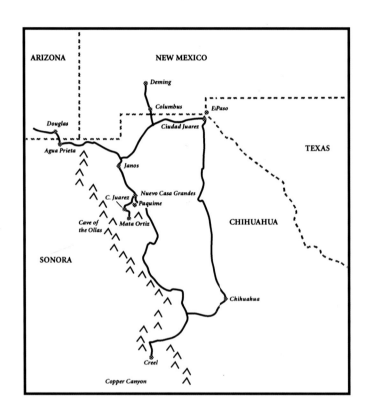

from the Tropic of Cancer across the modern border between Mexico and the United States as far as Colorado. Huge mountain ranges to the east and west created a north-south travel route without many internal barriers. This route extended north through the Gran Chichimeca and south, deep into Mesoamerica.

Paquimé

About 1000, A.D. a trading post was established in the Gran Chichimeca 150 miles south of the modern border, in what is now the Mexican state of Chihuahua. This grew into a major city and the center of the Casas Grandes ("large houses") culture. The Spanish gave the culture this name because of the huge ruined houses and buildings they found when they arrived in the late 1500's. The city they found was called Paquimé. ('Pah-ki-may). However, the Casas Grandes people were gone. Archaeologists excavated the site in the early 1960's, and for years have studied what they found. They cannot agree on where the people came from or where they went. Some believe that traveling

merchants, called "puchtecas," came north from Mesoamerica, established the trading center and spread the products and ideas of the more advanced southern cultures. Others argue that Paquimé was founded by religious rulers from the northern pueblo cultures in what is now the United States. No matter how it started, there is no doubt that Paquimé became a major trading center between the northern cultures and Mesoamerica. The archaeologists found storerooms full of trade items, including turquoise from Arizona, shells from the Pacific beaches, macaw feathers from the southern jungles, and copper ornaments made in Paquimé using Mesoamerican techniques.

One of the most important items found was pottery. The Casas Grandes people made ordinary pots for carrying water, cooking, and storing corn. But they also made fine thin-walled pots from the local white and yellow clays. These they painted with delicate red and black designs, some geometric and others of birds and snakes. Some of the designs were original and others reflected the influence of Mesoamerica, such as the plumed serpent representing the god Quetzalcoatl. (Ketz uh 'kwat tul) It was the broken pieces of these pots left behind by these ancient people that inspired Juan Quezada to begin experimenting with clay. (Walter P. Parks)

Modern Times

During the eighteenth and nineteenth centuries, the Apaches controlled parts of what is now Chihuahua, Sonora, Texas, New Mexico and Arizona. Geronimo, the last Apache warchief, played cat and mouse with United States Troops through this territory for sixteen months. In 1886, Geronimo surrendered. In Chihuahua, the Apaches continued a few more years under their war leader Victorio, until the military man Juan Mata Ortiz defeated them in the battle of Tres Castillos. This ended the Indian wars in the United States and Nothern Mexico.

In the early 1900's a lumber company began to harvest the forest in the Sierra Madre mountains above Mata Ortiz, a small village 20 miles south of Paquimé. The company created a thriving town and railroad complex until 1910, when Pancho Villa and the Mexican Revolution brought change in land distribution. By the 1960's the railroad, lumber company and most of the people had abandoned remote Mata Ortiz for opportunities elsewhere. Juan Quezada's family was one of the few that remained.

In 1976, when Spencer MacCallum knocked on Juan's door, Juan was 36. It had taken him twenty two years of experimenting to single-handedly revive the Casas Grandes pottery tradition. Juan thinks of his accomplishment as "a gift from God." Sharing this gift with his family and pueblo, he established the unique style of innovation that is the modern trademark of Mata Ortiz pottery.

WHERE DOES CLAY COME FROM?

Rain, wind and water wear down the earth's feldspathic rock. The rock decomposes, or breaks down, into clay. Colors are produced from the presence of metallic oxides, such as iron and copper (yellow, green, red), or manganese (brown, black).

Juan grinds each colored mineral rock in his *metate* with a *mano*. To make his *pinturas* Juan mixes the ground mineral color with water and a little of the same color *barro*. He paints this onto his *olla* with a brush made from a *nieta's* hair. Before the pot is fired, Guille burnishes it several times.

HOW DOES JUAN FIND CLAY?

Juan was using yellow and red clays by the time he was in his early twenties, but he wasn't able to locate the pure white clay he'd seen in the ancient shards.

When their children were small, Guille and Juan would walk far up the mountain with them for picnics. One afternoon, Juan noticed ants carrying tiny white lumps out of their tunnels. He walked over to the anthill and took a closer look. Quickly Juan dug a hole. The ants were carrying white clay! It was mixed with volcanic ash. He dug deeper, where more of the heavy clay had sunk into the lighter ash. Like river sand, ash opens up the clay body and prevents the clay from cracking. Ash from volcanoes is stronger in the fire and smoother to polish than gritty sand. Juan realized it is better to find clay with this natural mixture.

Today, Juan and his sons own the land where he collected firewood as a boy. He shares this perfect white vein and many other colored clay sources with all who want to dig. "Everywhere the sun shines is for everyone," he says.

K-6 LESSON PLAN

This lesson plan meets National Content Standards for K-6: Artistic Perception, Creative Expression, Historical and Cultural Context, and Aesthetic Valuing

OBJECTIVE: Use of <u>visual art elements</u> to evolve a personal design on a balloon "pot." Students will experiment with the art form perfected by Juan Quezada and Native Americans. They will research cultural symbols from long ago and today.

Shapes are created through the use of <u>line</u> to define contour or to create a <u>value</u> of light or dark by the <u>repetition</u> of lines. Emotion is created through gentle curves and symmetry, or harsh geometric lines and asymmetrical <u>balance</u>.

MATERIALS: per student

Tracing paper, soft charcoal, kneaded eraser, cereal bowl, small round white balloon, paint dish, water, 2 tablespoons black acrylic paint, or tempera paint mixed with liquid glue. Soft bristle long hair, thin watercolor brush, or: several strands 3" long medium-bodied hair from a student, duct taped to the sharpened end of a balsa wood chopstick, then cut evenly.

PROCEDURE:
1. Show images of Casas Grandes, Mata Ortiz and Native American designs to the class. Discuss what the symbols are based upon, and the significance of these objects within the respective cultures. If desired, include contemporary symbols, such as a handicap sign.

2. With charcoal on tracing paper, loosely trace or draw a continuous contour line, including inside patterns, of several favorite objects seen and used daily. Simplify by erasing parts of lines on each object, but keep the essence of the object's character. Experiment with several versions. Fill in any areas with <u>patterns</u> <u>of lines</u> to create <u>value</u> and impact. Young students paint over charcoal with black paint or other media.

3. Older students may continue by filling a balloon with enough water to keep it stable in the cereal bowl when inflated and tied. Lay the brush on the balloon and PULL it across the "pot" to draw the symbol. Using short strokes, fluid paint, and altering the symbol will lessen frustration. Encourage experimentation.

4. Discuss what a 25th c. archaeologist might deduct about the student's culture from their "pots."

THANKS

To original Norman, to June, Sascha, Craig, Arlo and Danielle for their continuous support

To Tom Fresh, Spencer MacCallum, Walter Parks, Herman and Marisa Knecthle, Rose Figueroa, Vanessa Acosta, and Teresa Mlawer for their patience and generous help with translating, photographs, history, travel, and for details that helped me to understand and share the story of Juan and Mata Ortiz.

To Juan and Guille, who invited me into their home and life as if I were family. This book is from Juan for the future generations of Mata Ortiz, and for children everywhere. What I've learned personally from Juan and the potters extends far beyond pottery.

To Chato, for not zinging me with his slingshot and for tolerating my photographing him.

To the people of Mata Ortiz, for their extraordinary hospitality.

For Terry

Text copyright © 2002 by Shelley Dale
Illustrations copyright © 2002 by Shelley Dale
All rights Reserved

ISBN 0-9708617-4-5
PCN 2001089950

Design by Rudy J. Ramos
Printed in Korea

9 8 7 6 5 4 3 2 1

The illustrations were done in watercolor, ink and colored pencil

Categories: art, artists, bilingual, biography, Casas Grandes, ceramics, Chihuahua, Educational, Hispanic and Latino, Juvenile non-fiction, Mata Ortiz, Mexico, oral history, pottery, pueblo, Quezada, Juan, Spanish, Standards, Storytelling.

Summary: Grandfather Juan, Grandmother and grandson make pottery while they share the telling of Juans' single-handed re-creation of the lost ceramic art of Casas Grandes, transforming their pueblo into a famous village of potters.

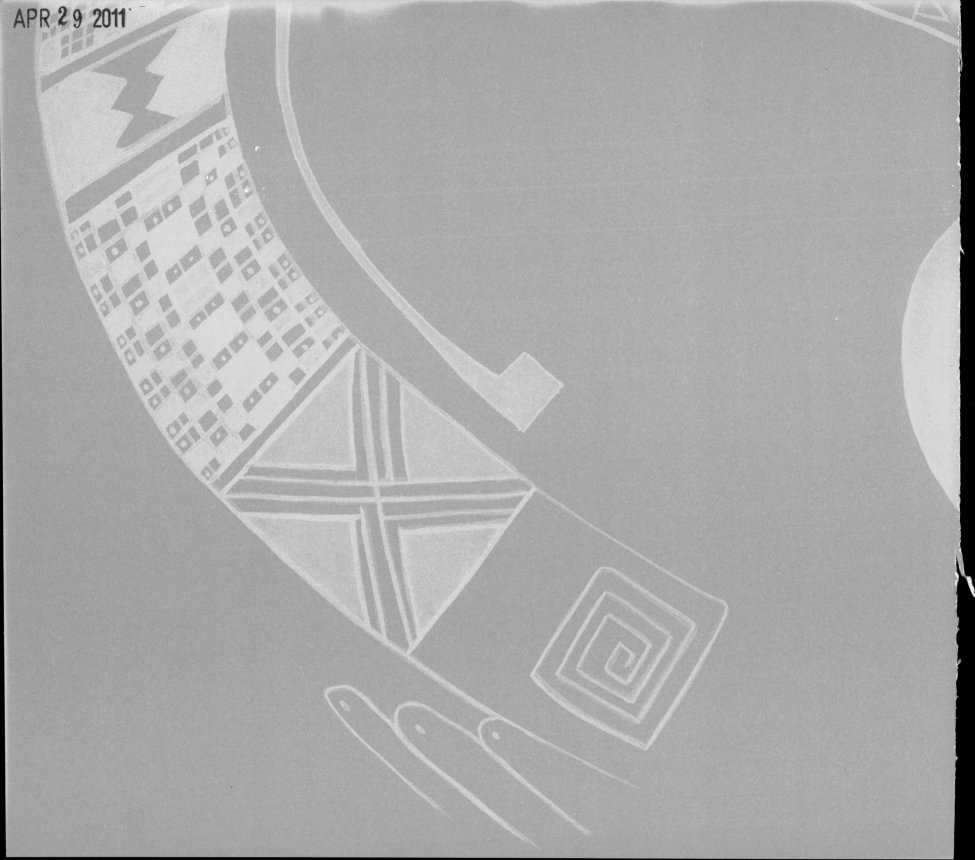